Chakras

Chakra Healing For Beginners: Achieve Equilibrium In Chakra Frequencies, Eliminate Obstructions, Enhance The Circulation Of Life Force Energy, And Sustain Harmonic Resonance

(An Infinite Quick-start Guide To Spiritual Awakening And Energy Healing)

Gert Kaindl

TABLE OF CONTENT

How To Clear The Chakra Of The Throat 1

The Eye Of The Third Chakra And Daily Life: Taking Care Of Your Third Eye 11

Using Colors Of The Third Eye In Your House 24

Meditations On The Solar Plexus (Manipura), Sacral, And Spine (Root) Chakras 37

Have Faith In Synchronicity, Felicity, And The Universe. 54

The Third Eye Chakra In Various Philosophical Traditions 83

The Historical Background Of Sex Magick 103

Energy: Recognizing And Correcting The 126

Committing To The Heart Chakra 147

How To Clear The Chakra Of The Throat

- Be mindful of your feelings on self-expression. Put on more blue to boost your self-expression confidence. Increase the amount of time you meditate on your throat chakra.
- Use blue crystals and gemstones to increase your self-confidence in your capacity for effective and clear communication. Blue topaz, lapis lazuli, blue sapphire, blue diamond, and blue lace agate are excellent jewelry and meditation choices.
- Every day following your meditation, perform a yoga pose that opens the throat chakra, such as shoulder stands. Always begin with a meditation that

focuses on opening your throat chakra by chanting "ham."

When it counts most, being aware of your sentiments and emotions can enable you to communicate them to others and yourself more effectively.

- Make an effort to communicate your emotions daily, and until your negative emotions are gone, try energizing them with more optimism.
- If you are afraid you won't finish a task, go ahead and finish it and deal with whatever prevents you from being truly successful.
- See a Reiki practitioner, discuss your concerns, and let them clear the chakra in your throat.

Consider your third eye chakra the source of your intuition, sixth sense, and psychic powers. It is located slightly above your eyebrows and is called Ajna (knowing, monitoring) in Sanskrit. You will feel more intuitive in all circumstances when your third eye chakra opens, and you will know things without realizing how you acquired the knowledge. Sounds eerie? It's eerie because you'll feel like you have superpowers when your third eye chakra is balanced. Your psychic sense might sometimes feel quite strong and open, particularly when it warns you about persons you might not be able to rely on or trust.

Additionally, if you are experiencing strong negative vibrations after making a decision that doesn't sit well with you, it would be in your best interest to reconsider. Through its extremely sensitive energy vortex, your third eye chakra is alerting you to this. Trusting your intuition is the secret to spiritual evolution and avoiding circumstances that are not advantageous or in your best interests. A balanced third eye chakra is primarily about following your intuition and trusting your gut. When you learn to trust your gut more often, you'll avoid finding yourself in needlessly uncomfortable circumstances. Consider how occasionally you can tell when someone around you is upset. Their emotions are sensed by your third eye chakra, which relays them back to you. That is how you can interpret circumstances. You are using the extrasensory abilities found in your third eye chakra.

Similarly, you'll be able to perceive and learn more about the spiritual and material realms. On the other hand, hypervigilance regarding extraterrestrial occurrences can also stem from an overactive third eye. Maintaining a balanced chakra requires finding equilibrium.

Put another way, maintain a strong spiritual connection to higher powers while being grounded in reality without getting overly fixated on them. It's crucial to embrace your instinct as second nature since it won't become underactive or hyperactive when you just notice, accept, and transcend it. Consider your sixth sense an inherent aspect of your identity and a natural means of connecting with your instincts to help you navigate life's path. By following your intuition, you might also learn how to get yourself out of difficult situations. This doesn't mean you should act badly toward people because you sense something negative from them, nor should you react emotionally because that will make you vulnerable. Instead, you should follow your gut without passing judgment on the circumstances and go with the flow—not necessarily the flow that other people are projecting or the flow that you feel you should be going with.

You should always do what makes you feel the most comfortable. You have an underactive third eye when you are less inclined to trust your psychic sense of "knowing" things that don't make sense to you right away. The mind does not exist in the spiritual world. You will only experience feelings due to your third eye chakra being open. Vibrations are indicative of these emotions. Even thoughts have vibrational frequencies, as you are already aware. We can perceive those ideas and the vibrations of unfulfilled future occurrences through our third eye chakra. Through this intuition.

You can only be aware of what is given to your attention through your third eye chakra; you cannot predict everything that will happen to you. Try it out and observe any visions or feelings that surface regarding other people when you are around them. Watch how things turn out. Have you ever thought of someone and then gotten a call or message from them, for instance? The third eye chakra is the source of the visions. In certain cases, you might even be able to sense the intentions of others toward you based on a vibration that their image or thought causes you to experience. You will feel more inner contentment and serenity when your third eye chakra is open and balanced.

When you start trusting your instincts, you can occasionally feel more intelligent. Feelings of empowerment and confidence will increase when you listen to and trust your intuition. Additionally, this will open the third eye chakra even more. Imagine a rich, deep indigo energy above your eyebrows that rises to the crown of your head. Inhale deeply this light, and as you do, feel the energy of wisdom and intuition coming in and going out. You will also sense a surge of trust and closeness to your higher self. Chanting or hearing the sound "aum" can help you open this energy center (Sahu, 2020).

The Eye Of The Third Chakra And Daily Life: Taking Care Of Your Third Eye

The quest does not end with pineal gland healing and third eye awakening. The third eye chakra needs constant balancing, strengthening, and nurturing to remain open and vibrant. Achieving your best self and improving yourself are ongoing projects for maintaining a healthy third eye chakra.

Fortunately, it's simple to incorporate these strategies and tactics into your daily routine. Whichever approach you choose, the objective is that it should become a habit that goes hand in hand with meditation. The result will be a strong and efficient habit enabling you to continuously cultivate your exceptional third eye.

Thriving Chakra: Eating Healthful Foods

The spiritual world is associated with the third eye chakra, not the material world. This could lead you to believe that it is unaffected by your dietary choices or physical activities. A few certain "superfoods" can maintain the balance and unblocking of the third eye chakra. Consuming a variety of these meals helps to maintain your perception open and your intuition robust.

The third eye also has a beauty resonance. It may surprise you that how you present your food on a plate and use color might stimulate your third eye. Fortunately, there is something for everyone on the extensive and diverse list of foods that support the health of the third eye chakra. You don't have to deny yourself or follow a rigorous diet. Ensure that you consume the maximum amount of the following foods:

1. Foods with indigo, violet, and purple hues are good for the pineal gland, which supports the third eye chakra. They are excellent blood pressure regulators and potent antioxidants that maintain the best possible brain health. Among them is Eggplant.

Purple grapes.

bluberries.

Fig.

Kale is purple.

Prunes.

Plums.

Onions in purple color.

Raisins.

Purple kale.

Lackberries.

These meals' color pigments stand for inner harmony with the universe, inner ideas, and dreams.

2. The hormone serotonin, which elevates mood, is found in dark chocolate and improves mental clarity. Try eating a slice before you start to increase concentration and enhance your meditation experience.

You can indulge in as much dark chocolate as you like as you work on opening your third eye chakra.

It should be noted that "dark" chocolate, not "milk" or "white," is the essential term here.

3. Rich in nutrients, nuts and seeds support clarity and attention in the brain. Almonds and pumpkin seeds are especially advised.

4. Omega-3 fatty acids, another excellent brain vitamin that improves focus and attention, are found in fish. When you open your third eye, try to consume fish at least twice a week; then, try to eat it once a week.

5. Spices and herbs uplift the senses and protect the nervous system. Strong flavors include mint, mugwort, juniper, rosemary, and poppy seeds. Since

ancient times, people have utilized turmeric to support general brain health.

6. Although it is common knowledge that we should drink lots of water, how many of us do so throughout the day? Maintaining mental clarity and attention. The greatest method for consistently flushing body toxins is to drink water. Prior to meditating, have a glass of water, as always.

Generally speaking, maintaining an open and balanced chakra system and overall greater health can be achieved by eating a smart, balanced diet rich in fresh fruits, vegetables, and healthy fats.

Nature and Exercise

This is an obvious choice. A harmonious chakra system results from a healthy body and mind. It's great that you are already participating in a certain sport or exercising.

Exercise in any form will maintain the flow of energy and the balance of your chakras. Nonetheless, you might want to think about engaging in the following active pursuits, which are particularly beneficial to third eye health:

Move. Dancing tones the body and enhances vision and creativity. All dancing forms, including dance-style aerobics, are good for the health of the third eye.

Gymnasium. Chakra balancing exercises that test your balance and coordination are great.

Yoga. The best physical activity for your third eye is yoga. This is so that a continuous energy flow between each chakra can occur. The exercises and poses used in yoga are designed to open up the chakra system. It also tones the body and encourages physical flexibility. If this speaks to you, consider enrolling in an introductory yoga session.

Nature. Any outdoor exercise that opens up your heart chakra is beneficial for the health of your third eye chakra. Cycling, hiking, swimming, climbing, and nature hikes are all excellent activities for fostering physical and mental well-being. You'll gain from the exercise, fresh air, and tranquility of being in nature.

Maintain a Dream Diary

One of the most important indicators that your third eye is open is psychic dreams. It awakens by sending vibrations through your system that facilitate the physical body's disconnection from dreaming so that dreams originate directly from the third eye.

While some people have clear memories of their dreams, others can recall very little or nothing.

You should anticipate having distinct memories of your dreams, though, as the third eye-opening makes the dream experience more vivid.

Keep a dream journal to monitor your dreams and identify any symbolic meanings. Examining the substance and progression of your dreams can also assist you in distinguishing between ordinary and psychic objectives.

Dreams: Normative or Psychic?

Many times, dreams are meaningless. Psychic visions are when our third eye gives precise messages about certain individuals or future happenings. When making plans, keep the following in mind:

Items that are meaningful or symbolic to you. The third eye is trying to tell you that the objective has changed.

Psychic dreams are shockingly vivid. You remember every little thing. Perhaps the next time you experience a dream this vivid, it will be a message from another world.

For this reason, keeping a dream notebook might be very beneficial. Reviewing the development of your dreams while your third eye chakra wakes is a great way to do this. You will be able to identify dream patterns and decipher dreams that deviate from their potential message-containing patterns.

Maintaining a dream journal as soon as you wake up takes several minutes every morning.

Encouraging enablement, jot down any personal symbolism you believe is pertinent and the meaning you associate with each dream.

When you cannot recall your dreams, note the date without making any entries.

Examine your entries once a week or twice and look for patterns, reoccurring symbols, or potential messages in your dreams.

iridescent light

Another name for it is Royal Blue. Indigo is associated with inner understanding and profound knowing, enabling us to discover special spiritual talents.

In order to nourish the third eye chakra with indigo light, we must turn to the night. The greatest time to expose your entire body to this striking hue is on a night under the stars or the moon. Observing the stars, moon, and stars while meditating beneath the night sky is the perfect way to experience indigo light's healing effect.

Using Colors Of The Third Eye In Your House

Deep blue and violet are combined to create the color indigo. You may guarantee that your third eye is always exposed to the related colors and their therapeutic vibrations by surrounding yourself with these hues in your home, office, and other personal spaces. Remember that the third eye chakra is related to beauty and finds its associated colors lovely. Therefore, this will keep it open and in good health.

Wherever you can use blue, purple, and indigo colors in your interior design, wall paintings, carpets, pillows, curtains, and bedspreads may all exhibit this. If you have an inexplicable affinity for these hues, you can use them for wall décor or furnishings.

You can wear jewelry with precious or semi-precious stones in indigo, dark blue, and purple and incorporate these colors into your outfit. Jewelry set with these stones is an excellent option because silver is the metal that resonates with the third eye the most.

Think about Beats in Two Dimensions

Soundtracks with binaural beats are intended to assist your brain in shifting into a particular wavelength condition. If you listened to them with headphones, that might be beneficial. The music is intended to play in two separate ways: one style is intended for the left ear, and one tone or sound frequency is intended for the right ear.

After processing the first two frequencies, the two tones assist Your brain in settling into the desired wavelength.

Binaural beats improve brain function, raise output, reduce anxiety and sadness, and enhance sleep quality. There's been some conflicting research on this type of "sound therapy," if you will.

But you might wish to experiment with binaural beats. By enabling the brain to vibrate at a lower frequency, binaural beats can promote third-eye chakra energy. Although it is unlikely that binaural beats will be extremely helpful, they might be ideal for you if you combine them with other practices like meditation.

The best approach is to try several frequencies and observe the results. You can find a variety of tracks on the internet and in inexpensive binaural beat applications.

Using aromatherapy

Essential oils are beautiful in a lot of ways. Though hundreds of studies have shown their therapeutic benefits, skeptics view them as a glorified scent. Since the brain and the olfactory nerves are closely linked, inhaled essential oils soon reach the affected area and begin to work their healing magic.

In addition to treating anxiety, reducing sadness, encouraging sleep, and sharpening focus, essential oils contain relaxing, stimulating, and pain-relieving properties.

Chapter 7: Vishuddha, the Throat Chakra

The base of your throat is home to the throat chakra. The translation from Sanskrit is to rid the body of impurities. This chakra is related to the element of ether or space. The Vedic philosophy holds that space was the first thing to be created. We have the chance to broaden our perspective because of the space.

Effective communication is the most often mentioned quality linked to this chakra. We can communicate the truth to ourselves and others thanks to the energy contained in this wheel. This chakra can support us in finding our creativity in addition to assisting with effective self-expression. It is the relationship that exists between our body language and speech. Because of its location, this chakra can be blocked by harmful food and contaminated air; nevertheless, when energy can flow through it, the body detoxifies and improved health is preserved.

The sixteen-petaled lotus is the throat chakra's symbol. These petals stand for various qualities, including pride, self-control, forgiveness, compassion, truthfulness, and directness. An upside-down triangle with a circle at the center is seen inside the lotus, representing the doorway to our spiritual development and consciousness. *Blue* is associated with stillness, communication, and a clear mind free of negativity.

You can communicate openly and honestly when your throat chakra is in equilibrium. You'll have faith in who you truly are and have an open mind. You will also improve as a listener in addition to this!

What You Can Learn From Your Throat Chakra

A large number of the physical symptoms are typical for this area of the body. Your speech can sound raspy, or you might get frequent sore throats. In more serious cases, you can have thyroid issues or laryngitis. Some people have gum disease and mouth ulcers. Some people have neck aches.

People with underactive throat chakra struggle to stand up for who they are, what they believe, or how they feel. Even though you may be aware of the limits you need and want to set, you may find it difficult to express them to others. You are likely unable to find the right words to describe your feelings. This gives you the impression that people don't understand you very well. The throat chakra may be blocked if you are anxious about revealing your actual feelings. Low self-esteem, an overwhelming tendency to use negative language, and the feeling that you are being conditioned by society rather than taking control of your destiny are more indications of a blocked neck chakra.

When the throat chakra is overactive, you can notice that you're gossiping, talking too much cut, turning others off, and interrupting others.

How to Take Care of Your Throat Chakra

Although deep breathing isn't typically associated with yoga, it can help release tension and energize your thyroids as you stretch. Deep breathing helps me let go of pent-up negativity and fill my lungs with pure, fresh oxygen!

Starting from a flat back position, place downward in the Supported Shoulderstand Pose (Salamba Sarvangasana).

With your feet hip-width apart, flex your knees and bring them close to your buttocks.

Gently raise your legs toward the ceiling while placing your hands on your lower back.

To raise your hips off the floor, firmly press your hands into your lower back.

Place your hands on your mid-back and use your palms to brace your spine.

Maintain a straight body while raising your legs toward the ceiling.

Tucked down and look up at your chest.

While taking steady, deep breaths.

Return your legs to the floor one at a time to release yourself from the pose.

Halasana, or Plow Pose: Start by lying flat on your back with your arms beside you and your palms facing downward.

Taking a breath, raise your legs toward the ceiling.

Breathe out, bend at the waist and slowly lower your legs behind your head.

Place your hands on your lower back to support your spine.

While taking steady, deep breaths.

Exhale, then gently roll each vertebrae slowly back down to the earth to release the pose.

It is necessary to place your knees exactly.

With your fingers pointing forward, spread your fingers wide and firmly plant your palms on the ground.

Keep your spine neutral and contract your core muscles.

Breathe in, arching your back slightly as you raise your chin, chest, and stomach toward the ceiling and lower your stomach toward the floor.

Take a breath, round your back, and tuck your chin close to your chest. Keep doing these two exercises, bringing your belly button toward your spine and synchronizing your breath with each one.

Meditations On The Solar Plexus (Manipura), Sacral, And Spine (Root) Chakras

Base Chakra

After allowing your eyes to close comfortably, calm your body and respiration, which will help your stomach and mind to settle.

Feel the richness of support beneath you, and then, as you connect with the earth, allow your weight to drop.

Recognize every sound around you and simply accept it as it is, without comment or judgment.

Feel the cool, gentle air gently brushing over the surface of your body. Notice the light and shadow that are coming in through your eyelashes.

Feel the earth beneath your feet, sustaining your body and weight and the vast expanses of sky above and below you.

To let your body let go and hold onto only what is necessary, let your thoughts entirely clean out anything that is no longer necessary and let it all freely depart your head, flowing far away.

Remove all thoughts of the day's events, tensions, aches, and frustrations from your mind. Bring the energy of your body to your center.

Now, start to look around you at the entire area. Breathe slowly, taking in all of this space while paying close attention to the rising and falling of your breath, the way it enters and exits your body, and the temperature, sound, and feelings of the space.

Breathe to your internal root, your distinct chakra of personal belonging, located directly beneath your spine, where your body's weight rests. Breathe into your root chakra. Then, as you gently extend your breath and let it become entirely soft, allow the energy of your life to fully nourish you.

Allow your root chakra to connect with the earth's interior. As the color of the earth, invite the color red into your being. Use red to fully activate your root chakra; this will ground, embody, and energize you in the here and now. Give your root chakra permission to absorb what it needs. Say, "This is where I am," "It is my right to be in this exact moment," and "I am supported and lived by the earth" to start.

When you're ready, let your awareness ascend to the Hara chakra, located directly below the navel, representing emotional intelligence, movement, and choice.

Incorporate air into your hara and let it soften, stretch, and expand as you breathe. This will allow the life force and revitalizing nourishment to enter your hara.

Remain conscious and pay close attention to how you are feeling right now. Right now, feel the warmth and affection that surround you. Let yourself rest in the knowledge that you are a singular entity.

Put an end to this meditation practice when you're ready.

Day 2: Take it easy. Allow your entire body to unwind and feel comfortable if you're lying on the floor. When seated, feel free to place your hands comfortably on your thighs or merely rest them on your side. Both postures are acceptable.

Close your eyes now. All of this time is set up just so for you. Release all of your worries. Allow your soul to effortlessly flow into the here and now. There is nothing outside of this very instant. Neither the past nor the future exists. There is only this time right now.

Drop and give your shoulders a break. Let your hands rest entirely. Allow your hair and eyes to be as serene as your face. Relax your jaw and provide your body's muscles with complete relaxation. Turn mushy.

Inhale a fresh breath. You'll be able to unwind and purify your soul by doing this. Release every bit of tension in your body. Allow your breathing to calm naturally. Fight the need to regulate your breathing. Simply pay attention to your thoughts, feelings, and breathing. Inhale and exhale deeply. Pay attention to the breathing pattern. Simply watch.

Now, direct your mental focus and attention to the base of your spine. Imagine a tiny red light circling, resembling a tiny whirlpool. Simply watch and take note of how it appears and feels. Develop an acute awareness of your breathing patterns. How quickly are you breathing? Is it moving more quickly or more slowly? In your body and soul. Inhale the crimson light into your body now. In the base chakra, sense this air. Watch as the red light expands outward and fills the base chakra. Take a breath and draw the crimson light toward you. This red light has a warm feel to it. Inhale deeply and exhale the stress. Repeat slowly and impartially but as a bystander.

Strong security, health, and strength are attracted to the red light. As this crimson light fills you, let it expand to your feet and experience the empowerment that comes from the light's complete connection to the earth's energy. Experience the red light's calming energy and calming effects. Take in the clean, peaceful spirit of the planet. Breathe self-assurance and personal security into your body. Release all of your fears from your soul. Remind yourself that you are in complete safety, spirit-in-tune.

It's time to shut down this chakra now. Focus exclusively on the tiny red light at the base of the chakra. Imagine this light getting smaller and smaller until it reaches the size of a thimble. Start the mantra now. The basic chakra is operating exactly as it should. "My spirit now approaches my earthly wants calmly, balanced. Every requirement I have is met in full.

Focus entirely on the inhalation and exhalation of the breath. Inhale and exhale deeply. As the cool breath enters your nostrils, it goes down to the back of your throat and expands fully into your lungs. Feel that cool breath. Pay attention to how the stomach naturally grows and contracts. Feel the floor beneath your body. Shrug your shoulders and feel your fingertips. Calmly open your eyes when you are all set.

Case studies

Sarah, a 23-year-old lady, has been battling an obstruction in her root chakra. Sarah's life had always seemed unstable and unsettling to her. She was constantly nervous, lacked self-assurance, and struggled to build solid foundations in her relationships, profession, and finances, among other areas of her life.

Sarah's childhood experiences of instability and lack of caring were the cause of her root chakra blockage. She had deep-seated concerns and uncertainties from her tumultuous upbringing, which impacted her sense of security and groundedness in the world.

After seeing how her blocked root chakra affected her whole health, Sarah set out on a healing path to clear the blockage and bring her energy center back into balance.

1. Awareness and Acknowledgment: Recognizing the underlying problems and their effects on Sarah's

life was the first step towards repairing her blocked root chakra. She was able to pinpoint the underlying reasons for her anxieties and insecurities and comprehend how they had influenced her beliefs and behavioral patterns through therapy and introspection.

2. Grounding Techniques: To re-establish a sense of stability and reconnect with the energy of the Earth, Sarah included grounding techniques in her daily routine. She started walking on the grass in her underwear, spending time in nature, and engaging in grounding exercises like deep breathing and visualization. Thanks to these

techniques, she could better anchor her energies and develop a greater connection to the present moment.

3. Physical Movement: Sarah participated in exercises that focused on stability and grounding to aid in healing her root chakra. She began to practice yoga, concentrating on warrior postures and Tadasana (mountain position), which are grounding poses. She felt more physically strong and stable and could release pent-up energy through regular activities like strength training and jogging.

4. Healing Modalities: Sarah investigated several healing modalities to release her root chakra blockage. In order to

address any energetic imbalances in her root chakra, she sought the assistance of an energy healer who conducted Reiki sessions. She also had regular acupuncture and massages, encouraging energy flow throughout her body and helping alleviate tension.

5. Emotional Release: Sarah used emotional healing techniques to let go of repressed feelings connected to her blocked root chakra. She took up journaling to communicate and let go of any pent-up anxieties, insecurities, or traumas from the past. She progressively released herself from the emotional weight dragging her

down due to this process, which helped her attain clarity and insight.
6. Self-nurturing and Self-Care: Sarah gave self-care routines that fed her body, mind, and soul top priority because she understood how important they were. She established a regular schedule for self-care that includes mindfulness exercises, soothing baths, nutritional foods, and establishing constructive boundaries in her relationships. These practices improved her general well-being, which assisted her in developing self-love and self-compassion.

Sarah's root chakra started to open and flow more freely as she became more dedicated to her recovery process.

Her life took a drastic turn for the better. She had less worry and gained more steadiness and self-assurance. She was able to make confident job decisions, build stronger and more satisfying relationships, and handle her finances more easily.

Through holistic healing techniques and addressing the underlying causes of her blockage, Sarah was able to effectively cure her blocked root chakra. She keeps incorporating these routines into her everyday life to preserve the stability and equilibrium she has built. Sarah's path shows the effectiveness of energetic healing, self-care, and self-awareness in balancing the chakras and improving general well-being.

Have Faith In Synchronicity, Felicity, And The Universe.

You must have faith in the mechanisms of the world around you, even though it will be difficult initially, particularly if you have never engaged in this kind of radical trust. You can learn much from others and yourself regarding personal development and healing. However, you can never fully anticipate the lessons the world and its greater forces can impart. Look up the terms "felicity," "synchronicity," and "serendipity." Once you begin searching for these experiences in your life, they will undoubtedly show up. In addition, I can nearly assure you that if you begin journaling about the synchronicities you encounter, you will soon be implementing tangible life adjustments and developing a greater sense of faith in the cosmos. Every contact, every sign you notice, is a lesson to be learned. Kundalini will know what to do if you open your eyes and learn how to trust again.

Become more aware of your breathing.

You'll become more aware of your breathing when you start meditation and eventually work it into your everyday routine. When you have the highest capacity for smelling, when you are urged to breathe gently when you are provoked, when you accidentally hold it, and more, you will notice. When you are aware of your breathing, your kundalini naturally reacts. One way to facilitate the process is to make an effort to meditate every day. During your meditation, take deep breaths into your abdomen.

Additionally, if you can envision, try to picture each breath as stroking the back of a tiny serpent dozing in your stomach's depths. As if you were petting a cat curled up in the window, picture the breath meeting the serpent. You will get healthier and more in tune with awakening due to paying ever-closer attention to your breathing.

Observe your posture more carefully.

Suppose you picture the path the kundalini serpent will take. In that case, you can see that it ascends from the root chakra to the sacrum, solar plexus, heart, throat, third eye, and crown before returning to the base and continuing as far as it can (assuming you are seated or standing upright). Imagine how the flow changes when you bend over and assume the fetal position. Chakra to chakra, the line gets curved, resembling a semicircle. The serpent's course is less predictable and more challenging in this instance. In this instance, you can assist the kundalini by being as aware of your posture as possible. Whenever feasible, try to sit up straight and stand up straight. Avoid squashing your root chakra and tucking in your solar plexus chakra if possible!

Moreover, consider which chakras can be restricted or blocked if you struggle with maintaining proper posture. Consider the traumas that might be impeding your progress. On your journey towards kundalini awakening, your posture may teach you a lot, no matter what you learn.

Attempt to open the "chakra channel." Specifically, try this technique in your everyday meditation. Though you don't have to, visualization can help the approach work just as well. You have to visualize the situation, keep your objectives in mind, and let your body take care of the rest. During the meditation, you will close your eyes and direct your energy toward the root chakra. Inhale deeply and focus on your lower abdomen, feeling the root chakra until you detect a vibration. Next, start reciting your mantra or just say "ohm" repeatedly. As the root energy flows into the sacral, solar plexus, heart, throat, third eye, and crown chakras, feel the vibration of the subsequent higher chakra with each repeat. Your entire chakra channel should pulsate with energy after reaching the crown. Your kundalini will undoubtedly view this cleared and open space as a possible playground to explore.

Learn to look for evidence of God's existence everywhere.

Try to change the way you see the world rather than shutting down when you're upset, getting furious at everything, or closing yourself off if you can; try to remember that even in the most intense moments, it's only a fleeting test from God that will only serve to strengthen you if you can appropriately and correctly channel it. Positive indications are similar to happy times and are frequently interpreted as evidence of God. The difficulty lies in the fact that bad and negative times are harder. With practice, I believe it will bring you both joy and enduring inspiration, as you will be able to recognize the evidence of divinity in every encounter, difficulty, benefit, circumstance, and trade. Your kundalini will benefit greatly; I'm sure of it (as long as you don't force yourself to feel a certain way in order to awaken).

Establish communication with your spirit guides.

To assist with your kundalini rising, you can attempt communicating with your spirit guides, whether they are actual individuals who are living or deceased, sainted, or extraordinary inventors, or if they are your ancestors or other real spirits. It is never shameful to ask for support, particularly for something as complicated and transformative as a kundalini awakening. Ask your guides for guidance. Tell them about your current circumstances and your goals. Share with them the issues and projects you're working on. It's time to start connecting with your spirit guides if you don't already know who they are. Consider the religion you most identify with and its "saints." Consider the gods and goddesses of the ancient faith you adore. See if your guides emerge by researching the spiritual community; if they do, you'll know to whom to address these crucial concerns centered around guidance.

Chapter 3: Root Chakra Healing

Why Is the Root Chakra Important, and What Does It Do?

The base of your body, directly above where you sit on the ground to meditate, is home to the root chakra. It is one of your primary "energy centers."

It promotes a loving, healthy relationship with yourself and others, a sense of connection to the natural world and groundedness. The root chakra gives us a strong connection to our physical needs and a profound connection with our bodies to take good care of them.

While karmic cleansing is frequently necessary to balance the root chakra, this does not imply that the chakra is "bad" or "wrong." You can anticipate experiencing difficulty grounding yourself or feeling deeply connected to the earth if your root chakra is out of balance. Ensuring your other chakras are balanced will help you get around this, but it's better to put in the effort than to cross your fingers. The root chakra also benefits you during meditation because it helps you become more grounded and conscious of what's happening inside your body and how you're projecting that onto others.

Generally, the root chakra is linked to our strong connection to nature and earthly belonging. It is closely related to emotions as well. More fully and profoundly, as well as to feel more rooted and connected to oneself. You may experience a deeper sense of connectedness to life and a greater sense of serenity with yourself and your surroundings.

The Effects of a Blocked Root Chakra on the Body

Back discomfort is the most typical physical result of a blocked root chakra. There are other physical effects as well. This is because your energy stays inside your body and concentrates on the problematic places when you're attached to the soil and your connection is blocked, making it impossible to take in or ground your energy. Other issues may include elevated blood pressure, lethargy and exhaustion, muscle strain, leg cramps, and more.

It's critical to balance the chakra before symptoms worsen since the longer it remains blocked, the higher the likelihood you may experience issues beyond simple discomfort. Your energy centers may begin to shut down due to your blocked root chakra. This might cause dullness around the soles of your feet, which can be extremely painful. In order to remove the obstruction and stop further energy loss, attempt to get help as soon as you can if you're experiencing this.

Consequences of a Blocked Root Chakra on Emotions

If you have a blocked root chakra, you should be able to track emotional issues back through your "energy centers" to this chakra, as this is typically where emotional issues begin. You may anticipate dealing with a variety of issues, such as anxiety and depression, as well as difficulties finding fulfillment in your career or relationships.

Additionally, you may find it difficult to communicate since you cannot articulate your deeper feelings or perhaps believe they are unreal. Finding what we're looking for often requires rediscovering our inner emotions, and occasionally, these feelings might impede our progress because we're too terrified of where they might go.

Anxiety, despair, or panic attacks might arise from feeling a little detached from oneself, which can be caused by an energy imbalance in the root chakra. With all the obstacles in your way, you can find it difficult to think properly, which could cause your thoughts to get confused. You may begin to feel unsatisfied with who you are or that life is meaningless. When this occurs, it might be difficult for you to trust anything, which can lead to uncertainty and anxiety. These thoughts can be difficult for the mind to process. It will, therefore, have an impact on your capacity to even move forward in the direction of your goals.

You will struggle to feel emotionally connected to people and grounded when your root chakra is obstructed. It may be difficult for you to feel connected to other people. You'll experience extreme detachment from the world or a sense of alienation as if no one can truly relate to you. This may lead you to make snap decisions, sometimes harmful. To be at peace with yourself and build relationships with others, it is advised to clear the root chakra if you are facing these issues.

Impact of a Blocked Root Chakra on Spirituality

You won't feel like you belong on this planet; thus, you'll find it hard to connect with anything spiritual if your root chakra is blocked. It's possible that you won't be able to sense the presence that precedes spiritual advancement or awakening.

It can be hard to believe in anything when it's blocked, but generally, you can have trouble believing in God or any other power. Even though you think well of yourself, you don't trust yourself, which makes it hard for you to fully open up and achieve your goals in life.

It's also possible to feel unmotivated and uninspired to do anything. Maintaining basic duties and feeling like there isn't enough "fire" in your soul to truly push yourself toward your goals can be difficult. This feeling can pass quickly at times, but if there is an energy blockage causing it, it will probably linger longer than most symptoms and complicate your life.

The Six Disorders of Anxiety

When someone encounters anything outside of their comfort zone, which can lead to many challenging situations, anxiety typically increases. For example, if you were about to give a lecture, go to an interview, or pass an exam. It affects people differently because while some may consider these situations typical, many others may find that they have a lasting effect on their entire lives, making it difficult for them to sleep, make mistakes at work, or properly eat. Anxiety specifically arises when the response deviates from what is often expected. It is possible to classify anxiety disorders into more specific types of disorders. These are the most common forms of anxiety.

Fear of spiders and panic attacks

Typically, this kind of anxiety begins as an uncontrollable panic attack and gradually expands to encompass fear of certain situations, such as driving, shopping, visiting new places, and being by yourself. This is mostly learned behavior. For example, you might experience a panic attack while driving, and this could exacerbate your anxiety going forward. Although the two may be unrelated, your mind has ingrained the connection.

Agoraphobia, also known as adult separation anxiety, is the fear of being alone and helpless in the face of extreme interior danger. This is frequently expressed as a fear of passing away, becoming insane, or losing control over one's behavior. Patients with agoraphobia may be more likely to stick close to people and places they are familiar with. It could get so bad that they stop going out of their house.

Particular Fear

One kind of situational anxiety is called a specific phobia, which includes claustrophobia, fear of heights, fear of insects or snakes, and dread of flying. It's not merely an act of fear; anxiety or panic are symptoms of actual terror. Phobias that are specific or isolated are situationally related and can be resolved by isolating themselves from an anxiety-inducing circumstance or circumstance. But what first seem to be distinct phobias are symptoms of agoraphobia that take the form of several phobias. Put another way, if you experience anxiety or panic during certain activities, you can have agoraphobia.

Fear of Social Situations

Pathological anxiety, known as social phobia, is characterized by a specific fear of shame, which might be limited to public speaking or can be a general timidity that prevents one from engaging in social activities, such as dating, marriage, and partnerships. Individuals who suffer from personal phobia frequently have low self-esteem and feel inadequate. These can be kids who have experienced bullying or overly cautious family members. People with personal phobias frequently prefer to be alone, whereas agoraphobics fear being by themselves.

Anxiety Disorder in General

Undoubtedly, general anxiety disorder (GAD) is a problem! Periods of extreme tension and anxiety are referred to as general anxiety. GAD's cumulative effects greatly impact the body. Those who experience a middle-age crisis or a nervous breakdown frequently have persistent GAD. Generally speaking, panic attacks, phobias, or pathological shyness are not present in people with GAD. It is the foundation of all anxiety disorders, but it does not guarantee that you will also have any other illnesses. An individual who appears tense or anxious all the time may have generalized anxiety.

Compulsive-Obsessive Disorder

Anxiety of this type is typically characterized by obsessions, which are undesirable thoughts that invade one's mind and are usually violent or sexual. Obsessive-compulsive disorder (OCD) sufferers are making an effort to get rid of these divisive thoughts. Engaging in compulsions, ritualistic nonsensical actions (e.g., repeating a phrase), or activity (e.g., hand washing, inspecting something, or following a precise route) might provide temporary respite from OCD-induced anxiety. OCD sufferers believe that their thoughts could hurt them or other people. The ideas are simply that—ideas—so it's not accurate.

trauma-related stress disorder

Anxiety brought on by a particularly stressful or drastically altering experience that a person has recently gone through is known as post-traumatic stress disorder. Some examples include being a part of a tragedy, a battle or brawl, the murder of a loved one, or a vicious crime. A person with PTSD may experience flashbacks that are so real they make them feel as though they are reliving the event. Someone with PTSD can use avoidance as a tool. For example, someone who has survived a plane accident will avoid airplanes and flights altogether.

Reasons for Uncertainty

Now that you are aware of how the anxiety system works. The origin of good anxiety is extremely obvious and straightforward: something actual is endangering your life, your health, or someone or something you love. In certain situations, the threat or danger is obvious and present! It's true; the horrible thing will happen, and now is the time to prepare for fight or flight. Almost anyone else in that same circumstance would experience worry and anxiety.

However, what triggers the various types of aberrant, severe anxiety that I have covered in this book thus far? Some believe that it's inherited or that it results from a past trauma that they spend weeks or months exploring in therapy. Others have been informed by their physician that taking antidepressants is the only way to correct a chemical imbalance in their brains.

As it happens, there are a plethora of potential reasons. The likelihood of experiencing anxiety and potentially even panic attacks increases with presence. Because of this, there isn't a magic bullet for anxiety or panic attacks. This is the reason why drugs don't provide sufficient long-term effects. This is also why scouring your past for the root of the problem won't help you much either. Anxiety is brought on by a variety of tiny factors that, when added together, will make you grin broadly.

Before we get into the main anxiety busters in part two, I'll go over these causes, critique some fallacious arguments that you shouldn't listen to, and provide some coping mechanisms in the following sections. It's almost here.

I want to emphasize that you are not flawed in any way. You may have questioned why you don't have anxiety like other individuals who appear to be always happy, socialize, have amazing experiences, and never seem to have any problems. We are both aware that those folks only post flawless, frequently scripted moments from their lives. Nobody has the ideal life or feels flawless all the time. There are people out there who are more adept at managing anxiety than you are right now.

When you read what follows and understand that I'm talking about you or something you do, please write it down. It would be best if you wrote it in a diary that you will use for this book. One of your causes will be what you identify and record; you must keep an eye on this cause while you work to overcome your unwelcome uneasiness. Anxiety is pushed toward by every source to some degree (some more than others). The likelihood of having panic episodes and developing an anxiety disorder increases with the number of contributing factors. The skies will once again be brighter the more reasons you remove.

The Third Eye Chakra In Various Philosophical Traditions

Numerous civilizations and traditions have accepted the third eye as a crucial component of the spiritual path. Let's examine these civilizations in more detail.

Hinduism

The third eye is closely associated with Lord Shiva in Hinduism. Based on Sanskrit, the word ajna means "command" and "foremost." Stated differently, the third eye is the main location of awareness and intuition. This chakra can also serve as a control center for various mental, emotional, and spiritual activities. It is situated in the head. Ajna, pronounced agya, also translates as "beyond wisdom." In Hindu tradition, the third eye is believed to be located on the forehead, and a tika or tilak is applied there—typically following morning prayers. The tilak is a tiny, typically crimson mark applied to the chakra of the third eye. The third eye chakra's energy is said to be preserved when it is lightly touched and covered with tilak. It should also support knowledge and focus as we meet the day's obligations.

The third eye, often called the urna, is initially observed in Lord Shiva.

The third eye possesses the ability to see past illusion and into reality. It is also interpreted as a symbol of both defense and destruction. Shiva is revered as the Destroyer and is renowned for shielding his devotees from evil. Indeed, legend has it that the world as we know it will end when Shiva opens his third eye. It can be difficult to deal with for someone who doesn't get the spiritual meaning of this.

The legend states that as Shiva pursued his goal of becoming the Adiyogi, the god of Lust, Kamadeva, fired an arrow into his heart. At that moment, Kamadeva was reduced to ashes by Shiva, who then opened his third eye. This can appear to be a frightening interpretation of the third eye's ability, as you might expect.

But we must comprehend the meaning behind this. In this context, Lust refers to any desire we may ever have. It is nearly difficult for humans to live without desires. Our passion for something inspires us to work toward achieving it. It also goes by the names of ambition and desire, which are ideas that drive us to pursue goals in life. We might as well not have a mission if we lack desire. The problem is that these wants are typically, if not always, materialistic. We frequently don't even know if we want the things we are pursuing in life.

Usually, desires stem from feelings of inadequacy. We can't be content with what we have as long as we're looking for the next big thing. Since desires have no boundaries, we can feel inadequate for our entire lives. Being faithful to your soul's purpose is not the same as this. Shiva wanted to become a master of yoga so that he might comprehend the inherent essence of reality. Any aspirations that got in the way of him were from within, not from outside. This is the portion that requires our attention.

When we first start a spiritual practice, it's simple to blame outside factors for our diversion. In actuality, we are the ones who inadvertently put roadblocks in our way. Thus, Shiva truly destroys everything within himself that prevents him from realizing the reality of this world and the one beyond when he "destroys" Kama. For this reason, the third eye is believed to allow us to look within. Stated differently, we already own what we need; this journey only facilitates our acceptance of this reality.

In the fourth chapter, we'll further detail the relationship between the third eye and intuition.

Buddhism

Buddhists believe that the third eye plays a critical role in assisting humanity in putting an end to its suffering. This school of thinking, similar to the Hindu school, holds that an aligned third eye raises the practitioner's consciousness. This lets us see reality through the "eye of the soul," transcending the material world.

Sacred Tibetan Buddhist paintings known as thangkas typically feature a third eye on the foreheads of the deities. It represents how the third eye opens up and transforms into the "wisdom eye" in any enlightened being.

The third eye alignment is associated with acquiring knowledge, which is one of the three primary teachings of Buddha: discipline, meditation, and wisdom. The teachings state that the only way to become wise is to have the "Right View," which is the capacity to recognize the absolute truth instead of the relative truth.

Put another way, the awakening of the third eye chakra is directly linked to the capacity to see reality rather than as it is presented to us due to our failings.

Chinese philosophy

The notion of prana is not exclusive to Buddhism and Hinduism. The life energy that is essential to Taoist teachings is called qi. Like pranayama, which is the practice of regulating and utilizing prana, the "microcosmic orbit" is a Taoist meditation method that facilitates regulating energy flow via the subtle body. There is a close connection between this practice and the third eye notion.

In Taoist practices, inner vigor, spiritual awareness, and intuition are associated with the third eye. Taoist teachings emphasize the significance of energy work, mindfulness, and meditation to align our third eye chakra, much like Hindu and Buddhist traditions do.

Mythology of Egypt

The emblem, also called the Eye of Horus, is associated with the third eye in Egyptian mythology. The Egyptian deity Horus, representing the sky, combat, and protection, is linked to this eye. The Eye of Horus is seen as a representation of strength, protection, prosperity, and good health. It also has to do with healing, rebirth, and renewal. Recalling the relationship between light and the third eye, this symbol is associated with illumination and is frequently interpreted as the sun.

It is shown as the "all-seeing eye" as well. Artifacts and even tombs from the ancient Egyptians bear this emblem. One fascinating feature of this symbol is that its many components line up with the areas of the brain that regulate perception when superimposed over an image of the human brain. Just as our senses aid in our understanding of the outside world, the Eye of Horus enhances our capacity for perception.

EXTENSIVE MULADHARA CHAKRA DEEPLY

Place it in a cozy position. With one leg resting on top of the other, cross your legs. If you cannot sit cross-legged, you can sit however comfortable, even on a hard surface. Maintain a straight spine. Head and spine in alignment.

(Hold off for ten seconds.)

Through your spine, energy flows upward from the lowest chakra to the highest chakra. It is vital that the energy, or kundalini Shakti, can flow freely through your posture.

Shut your eyes gently. Hold out your hand in the chin mudra. Your hands should be lightly placed on your knees in the chin mudra. Maintaining the other fingers straight, lightly connect the thumb's tip with the index finger's tip.

(Hold off for ten seconds.)

You have a straight elbow position. Avoid applying any force to your hands or fingers. Muladhara, the base chakra, is connected to the chin mudra. Except for the idea that you will clear and cure the Muladhara chakra, gently eliminate every other concept from your mind.

(Hold off for ten seconds.)

Your breathing is regular. Your tummy expands when you inhale and contracts when you exhale. As warm air from your nostrils and cool air enters, sense these changes.

Your Prana Shakti heats the air you breathe. The life-giving energy heats your breathing and body.

It must have occurred to you that dead bodies get cold. The prana, or life-giving energy, departs the body during death. Chakras are gently and gradually activated, unblocked, and healed. It can only be done when your body and mind are in a solid and constant state.

Imagine momentarily that you will clear the pranic energy from your Muladhara chakra and cure it.

(Stop for ten seconds) At this point, the Muladhara chakra has to be cleared and healed.

The Muladhara represents the ground. It has a red color to it. The earth is a metaphor for steadiness and substance. There is a sharp release of energy as this chakra opens. A throbbing energy that nourishes and revitalizes you greets you when you arise. It stays latent and inert when obstructed.

There are two layers to sensations, feelings, and experiences: the physical and the mental. You can become gloomy and experience anxiety and depression when you have heavy thoughts. An incoherent mind cannot function well. You don't accomplish anything because of fear and anxiety. You just sit around doing nothing.

Your mental indifference causes physical imbalance and illness. Your body releases toxic hormones and chemicals in response to unfavorable emotions. You become vulnerable to diseases and pollution as a result.

To ensure a fruitful existence, mind and body healing is necessary. This energetic state is only accessible upon clearing and healing the Muladhara chakra.

(Take a two-second break.)

Now, to clear this important chakra, you will do two exercises: physical and mental.

The Root Lock, also known as Mula Bandha, is the first exercise. The chakra in men is situated in the perineum, which is the area between the genitalia and the anus. It is situated close to the cervix's opening in females.

Now, picture the Muladhara chakra center, which is situated at your backbone.

(Stop for five seconds.)

Inhale deeply. Constrict your pelvic region as you inhale. For as long as the contraction lasts, hold your breath. You might only be able to hold the contraction for a short while at first.

(Hold off for ten seconds.)

Your pelvic muscles contract during inhalation, causing your lower body to slightly elevate. The contractions are similar to the tone of your muscles when you try to control the passing of feces or pee.

You should just squeeze the area around your pelvis, not your buttocks. Breathe out softly and let your pelvic muscles relax. Inhaling makes it simpler to constrict the Muladhara chakra. You can hold the contraction while breathing if you feel this helps.

(Hold off for ten seconds.)

Ten times over, perform the Mula Bandha exercise. The length of the contractions can be increased from a few seconds to over a minute.

(Hold off for a minute.)

The Muladhara chakra remains latent and inactive if the pelvis muscles are not toned. This causes you to become lethargic and inactive. You are reviving the dormant energy within yourself by strengthening the muscles at the Muladhara chakra location.

After practicing Mula Bandha for a few days, you will sense a new vitality. You'll become motivated and start moving. You can also have premature ejaculation and erectile dysfunction when the Muladhara chakra is out of balance. This occurs as a result of your pelvic muscles contracting against your will.

You will be pleasantly delighted to have more heightened sexual pleasure after practicing Mula Bandha. A normal component of both physical and mental health is sex. Numerous powerful hormones that calm and revitalize you are released when you experience sexual pleasure. A life out of harmony is invariably the result of an unhappy sexual life.

A rise in self-assurance results from the Muladhara chakra's contraction and release. This method of energizing the Muladhara chakra unlocks dormant energy that would otherwise evaporate.

The Historical Background Of Sex Magick

Embark on a voyage into the past that will reveal the sex magick's ancient roots and engross you in the mysterious realm of its magical history. This chapter will take us on an engrossing journey into the historical significance of sex magick, revealing its enormous influence on spiritual practices, faiths, and societies throughout history.

Imagine traveling back in time and finding yourself in front of the magnificent temples of bygone eras. As you go into the mysterious initiation zone, where the esoteric knowledge of sex magick was whispered among the chosen few, you can feel the sacredness in the air. These prehistoric cultures understood the tremendous potential inherent in human sexuality and worked to harness it for both individual and group transformation.

Examining its Historical Significance and Mythical Origins

Ancient Mesopotamia was one society that valued the power of sexual energy. Priestesses and priests carried out rites honoring the divine union of male and feminine elements in the sacred temples of Sumeria and Babylon. They realized that one might access the earliest energies of creation and direct them toward spiritual development and manifestation using sexual energy.

We travel on and come to the ancient Egyptians, who had an unshakeable respect for the fusion of spirituality and sensuality. The story of Osiris and Isis represents their belief in the cyclical cycle of life and death. This holy couple embodied the holy union of male and feminine forces and represented the perpetual unity of opposites. Temples devoted to the goddess Hathor honored sexuality's creative potential and function in uniting the divine and the mundane.

We are therefore drawn to the knowledge of the tantric traditions, with its deep insight into sexual energy as a means of achieving spiritual enlightenment. Tantra, which has its roots in ancient India, saw sexual connection as a sacred act that might transcend sensual pleasure and result in very spiritual experiences. Practitioners developed their sexual energy through a set of rites and practices that allowed it to flow smoothly throughout the body, reawakening latent spiritual abilities and achieving states of sublime ecstasy.

After traversing enormous continents, we arrive at ancient China, where Taoist beliefs valued the interaction of yin and yang energy. The Taoist sages understood the potency of sexual energy and its essential function in preserving emotional, mental, and spiritual equilibrium. Techniques like the "inner smile" and "microcosmic orbit" helped practitioners to nourish the organs and promote spiritual awakening by circulating sexual energy throughout the body.

We come upon the wisdom of old Indian scriptures, such as the Kama Sutra, when we travel through time. Regarded as a manual for leading a happy life, the Kama Sutra provides insights into the spiritual aspects of sexuality in addition to helpful guidance on sexual practices. It acknowledges that, when treated with compassion, attention, and respect, sexual energy can be a powerful force for pleasure, connection, and personal development.

The adoration of Aphrodite led the ancient Greeks, known for appreciating beauty and sensuality, to investigate the domains of sex magick. Priestesses celebrated ecstasy and sexual pleasure via ceremonies in the sacred rites of the goddess of love. Through these activities, people could transcend social constraints and achieve altered levels of awareness, realizing the divine essence of their sensuality.

The discovery of esoteric knowledge and alchemy during the Middle Ages created a conducive environment for the study of sex magick. Alchemists combined the conflicting forces of feminine and male energy inside themselves to discover the universe's secrets. They held that one might achieve spiritual enlightenment by symbolically marrying these powers in an alchemical manner and turning base components into pure gold.

Sex magic's historical relevance extended beyond the Middle Ages and ancient civilizations. It found a home in the many spiritual traditions that developed in the following centuries. For example, Gnosticism acknowledged the close relationship between spiritual understanding and sexuality. Gnostics accepted the transforming potential of sexual union as a way to pass beyond the bounds of the physical world and enter higher states of awareness in their pursuit of gnosis or spiritual knowledge.

Another mystical school, hermeticism, saw the oneness of all things and considered sexual energy essential to spiritual development. It recognized that balancing one's sexual powers may help one align with divine energies that are present everywhere, which could lead to mystical experiences and personal development.

Sex magic saw a rise in popularity throughout the Renaissance as occultists and alchemists tried to unlock the mysteries of creation. The information about this ancient technique was expanded by individuals like Heinrich Cornelius Agrippa, who studied the esoteric teachings of sex magick, and Paracelsus, who was deeply aware of the relationship between nature and the human body.

Sex magic has made a lasting impression on society throughout the years. It has influenced the stories of old myths, stoked the creative energies of poets and painters, and influenced seekers' ambitions toward enlightenment. Its tremendous influence on investigating human potential, the comprehension of sexuality, and the quest for spiritual enlightenment make it historically significant in addition to its esoteric teachings.

We are encouraged to establish a connection with the knowledge and customs of our ancestors as we explore the historical roots of sex magick. The timeless truths of this mystical art still speak to people today who are looking to harness the transformational power of spirituality and sexuality as we stand at a crossroads in history.

We'll look at useful methods, customs, and insights in the upcoming chapters to guide you through the world of sex magick. We will explore the subtleties of using sex as a tool for spiritual and personal development, drawing in partners who share our desires, and using the alchemical combination of sex and magick to realize our dreams.

Come explore the historical roots of sex magick with me, and let the wisdom of our ancestors lead us on a journey of transcendence, empowerment, and self-discovery. As we accept the eternal wisdom this sacred practice brings to those who dare to explore its mysterious depths, let us also honor its historical significance. Let's go out on a trip together that will heighten our senses, broaden our awareness, and reveal the transformational potential of sex magick.

Chapter 1: "The Journey of the Soul"

Only when one comprehends the universe's operational pattern can victory be declared.

Failure awaits those who struggle against the universe's design without comprehending its functioning principles. Yes, I am referring to the universal working principle, which holds true for every individual in the universe.

There are a lot of unknowing forces in this society that use us as puppets. We can absorb everything once we comprehend it.

When he observed an apple fall straight to the earth, Isaac Newton questioned why it did not fall vertically or horizontally. He subsequently tried to comprehend this occurrence and established the definition of gravity. The law of gravity was the basis for numerous beneficial inventions for humanity.

The law of gravitation was known before humans were. But since we were unaware of it, we could not benefit from it. We were able to benefit from it once we comprehended it.

In a similar vein, we are ignorant of a great deal of existing theories.

But when we comprehend and obey the principles of nature, we come up with amazing technologies that help us succeed.

Ignorance of the natural laws might cause obstacles in one's path or even bring one to ruin. Sometimes, even though we know nature's rules, we lack the strength, power, or capacity to put them into practice.

What has man not accomplished, from radio to telephone, television to computer, automobile to airplane, lightbulb to moon? What failed to produce? Then why is this powerful individual unhappy with his life? Why does he not seem content? Why, after all this, is he still hungry for more? What else is there to know? What is still unclear? Are we attempting to suggest that happiness remains elusive despite humanity's material accomplishments?

Let's attempt to comprehend a few natural rules that can lead to prosperity and happiness in life. The author, Ganesh Karapu, has improved his and many others' lives by putting these ideas into practice. The entire work is based on his own experiences.

NOW IS WHEN THE WAIT ENDS!

Let's begin with a brief work of fiction to fully understand the author's point of view and what he is trying to convey.

Suddenly, a man found himself aboard a little. Someone who lacks knowledge about their past, origins, or plans and is unsure where to go. He doesn't realize where he is at this moment. He has no idea who he is! (As if someone had just awakened from a coma and lost all recollection). Waves are heaving his boat, and his main concern is getting himself to safety and land.

He waits for many days in the middle of the sea, paddling the boat with his hands when not a single coast is in sight, not a single soul is in sight, and there is no support for him to live. No guidance, no hope, and no remedy. There is fear and waiting all the time.

Living in constant fear, he eventually learns to adjust to the waves. After many days of waiting and laboring, tormented by hunger and thirst, he finally reaches a shore. He is clueless about the location, how he got there, and where he needs to go next.

He gently begins to walk a little farther as soon as he touches the shore, and soon, a route takes him directly into a dangerous woodland. That woodland is home to a great number of feared animals as well as several little species. There are fruits to be eaten and river water to drink somewhere.

Numerous hazardous animals attack him as he goes forward. He takes off running in an attempt to save himself. He sometimes attacks animals in order to defend himself.

As time passes, he begins to look for himself in the bush. What location is he at? What has brought him there? Who is this guy? What direction should he go? Years go by as this quest is conducted. He sometimes avoids these queries because he is too sleepy. Because there are situations when this question persists even when it is not fully understood. He always asks himself, "Who am I, and where am I from?"

He becomes fatigued and unwell at different times. There are moments when the loneliness he felt followed him around. There is no right or wrong path in his life right now. After years of searching, he stumbles into a hermitage while out for a stroll when he witnesses an elderly man performing penance. The old guy uses his heavenly knowledge to teach the man everything he needs to know about himself, his life, and his mission as soon as he arrives at the ashram. He then begins a new life with a new mission after that. His wait is over, and his life turns into a party.

In the same way, sometimes we see our own lives reflected in the lives of many others, and we experience just this. What is life? We question ourselves occasionally. What is our life's purpose? In what direction is our life headed? When will it be possible for us to let go of our grief?

Just consider the home where we were born, our upbringing, and our early years. We had no idea who we were. Where did we originate from prior to this birth? Why are we here? When this existence ends, where shall we go? We think we comprehend ourselves at times. We often ask ourselves, "Why does this keep happening to us?" occasionally, we think we can accomplish a lot, so we keep working hard and occasionally choose the incorrect route to get where we want to go faster because we don't know how to get there.

Only 10% of individuals on the planet truly grasp who they are, their purpose, or how to solve their problems. The remainder put in a lot of effort and do it with genuine love. The remaining 90% of people live like a frog in a well. They combat illnesses and issues with their narrow minds, losing their precious lives in the process.

Unaware of who they are, they combat issues until the end of their existence between birth and death. They have no idea where they are or even where to go. We'll just talk about arriving and going, but how many people are pleased with their lives right now?

We represent the 10% of individuals constantly looking for the Truth. Attempting to comprehend who we are. We age, and time passes, but we never give up on our search. We never stop looking for answers to questions about who we are, why we exist, and our ultimate objective. When we finally hold a book like this during this quest, it feels like the wait is done. We do not doubt that a fresh life with a different viewpoint will begin after reading this book.

Energy: Recognizing And Correcting The Chakras

The Sanskrit term "chakra" means "wheel" or "cycle." The body contains twelve chakras, or energy centers, of which seven are significant, and five are minor. We'll concentrate on the seven main chakras for our purposes, which run from the base of the spine (tailbone) to the crown of the head. There is a corresponding color for each chakra, forming an ascending rainbow. Spiritual practices like yoga view the chakras as energy centers shaped like wheels that are not visible to the naked eye but are part of the subtle spiritual body and interact with the physical body.

An energy channel that runs the length of the spine connects the seven chakras. Numerous functions, such as the immune system, organ function, and even our emotions, are regulated by this energy flow. In addition to having a corresponding organ and gland, each chakra is a portal for the human form. First, chakra is associated with outward appearance; second, with the ability to create; third, with emotions; fourth, with love; fifth, with expression; sixth, intellect, intuition, and reasoning; and seventh, with the spiritual quality of unity. Furthermore, the chakras are good health, wellbeing, and wellbeing markers. These whirling energy vortices can transmit energy from the cosmos to balance and align the body when the chakras align.

Because of our upbringing, education, and experiences, certain facets of our identity have evolved more than others. Consequently, certain chakras will be open and in good health. Some will be barred; these are accessible, but not all are healthy. Others will be closed, which means they are not operational. Diseases of the body and mind can develop from these imbalances, but happiness, wholeness, and wellbeing result from having everything in balance.

Chakras are energy sites that, in short, maintain mental and physical equilibrium in the body. They establish connections between our emotional, spiritual, biological, and psychological selves.

The Seven Spiritual Branches

Copyright 2023 Jane W. N.

You can locate your energy centers and harmonize and balance them with various modalities, including dancing, active and passive meditation, and rebirth, a therapeutic method focused on conscious breathing. A brief description of each chakra is given here, along with its Sanskrit name in parenthesis.

The Root or First Chakra (Mūlādhāra)

The initial energy center forms your core and the start of your development. Its energy begins at conception and lasts during the cell division during the embryonic stage. Organ development follows the development of the spinal column, which starts at the root chakra and progresses to the crown chakra.

Your innate response from birth is the result of the root chakra. Because of this, your animal nature is controlled by your basic sensations of taste and smell, and the survival center triggers the fight, flee, or freeze reaction. For this reason, infants turn their heads to sniff and then taste for food, a process known as rooting. The infant acknowledges that they are a part of the world and that people would support their survival this way.

Children learn to trust that they are in the proper location when they get constant affirmation of their existence, such as nourishment, love, affection, and quiet. A child who receives inconsistent assistance will grow up afraid, insecure, and lacking trust. How safe you feel as a youngster determines how secure and trustworthy you feel now.

You'll find the root chakra at the base of the spine or close to the tailbone. Since the root chakra is the heaviest of the energy centers, it is typically symbolized by red, the densest color. The most stimulating color, red, causes the retina in your eye to move forward, focusing your energy and attention outward. You, therefore, cannot feel your energies and concentrate inward when you are in survival mode. Red is the universal color for Stop because it attracts attention. Red also has a lot of energy, suggesting it will survive.

The root chakra is associated with energy and survival and is linked to the earth element, which connects your body, surroundings, and the earth. Physical characteristics, including the intestines, kidneys, skeleton, bones, muscles, and adrenal glands, are linked to this energy center. This chakra is also connected to the left atrial blood chamber of the heart, which pumps blood containing nutrients and oxygen to your body's tissues. Your motivation to eat, sleep, co-create, grow in integrity, and feel brave comes from your root chakra. It helps you feel rooted in the land and linked to others, giving you a sense of belonging.

You can connect with your ancestors' spiritual energies, victories, and struggles through this energy center. Many of us have root chakra imbalances or problems due to these ancestral experiences. The root chakra's energies contain memories of hunger, war, and other traumatic incidents that endanger our lives. This applies to all generational seeds of ideas, goals, and deeds ingrained in our life force and transmitted from generation to generation, unintentionally forming generational patterns. You and your offspring can break free from these patterns and forge new paths in life by consciously and persistently working on the energy centers.

This chakra is associated with the elements that give you a sense of grounding, including food, water, shelter, safety, fearlessness, and attending to your emotional needs. You feel more comfortable and secure when these demands are met. When this chakra is balanced or aligned, you possess bravery, a strong will to life, and inventiveness.

This chakra is associated with the spine and the digestive system. Lack of energy, back discomfort, frigid feelings, insecurity, mistrust, sexual issues, constipation, and aggression can all be caused by any blockage or imbalance. A balanced diet, working with the earth (gardening, going outside barefoot, etc.), wearing red clothing, consuming red foods (strawberries, tomatoes, lean red meat from grass-fed cattle, etc.), practicing meditation, working out, dancing, and generally moving your body are the most effective ways to rebalance the root chakra. This chakra influences every other chakra due to its high energy density.

Chapter 1: Chakra Interpretation

This chapter will thoroughly understand chakras and how they affect our mental, emotional, and spiritual health, laying the groundwork for your journey into chakra healing. Gaining a greater understanding of these energy centers will make it easier for you to navigate the upcoming chapters and practice chakra healing with assurance and clarity.

The Chakra System's History:

Ancient Indian spiritual traditions, particularly those of yoga and Ayurveda, have a rich history with chakras. These spinning energy wheels are considered essential centers in our subtle body, in charge of the distribution and circulation of prana, or life force energy.

The System of Chakras:

The seven primary chakras that make up the chakra system are arranged from the base of the spine to the top of the head along the body's center channel. Every chakra influences our mental, emotional, and spiritual states. It is linked to particular attributes, components, colors, and functions.

Chakras and Energy Flow: Throughout our entire being, our chakras act as entry points for energy flow. Energy flows freely and promotes health and wellbeing when our chakras are open and balanced. On the other hand, chakra blockages or imbalances can interfere with the flow of energy and cause emotional difficulties, physical illnesses, and separation.

The Primary Seven Chakras:

Let's take a closer look at each of the seven primary chakras, working our way up from the base of the spine:

At the base of the spine, it is connected to our survival instincts and sense of stability. It is associated with the earth element and symbolized by red.

The sacral chakra, also known as the svadhishthana, is located in the lower belly and is associated with creativity, sexuality, and emotional health.

Solar Plexus Chakra (Manipura): This chakra, situated in the upper abdomen, is in charge of our willpower, self-assurance, and inner strength. It is symbolized by yellow and is related to the element of fire.

Heart Chakra (Anahata): The heart chakra connects the upper and lower chakras in the middle of the chest. It controls our capacity for love, forgiveness, and compassion. It is symbolized by the color green and is associated with the element of air.

Throat Chakra (Vishuddha): Located at the throat, this expresses ourselves and speaks authentically. It is associated with the sound element and is symbolized by the color blue.

Third Eye Chakra (Ajna):

Situated at the top of the head, it symbolizes our link to higher states of consciousness, spiritual awareness, and divine consciousness. It is associated with the element of mind and is symbolized by either white or violet.

Chakra Imbalances and Blockages: Stress, trauma, negative emotions, poor lifestyle choices, and energetic disturbances are a few of the variables that can cause imbalances or blockages in the chakras. Physical illnesses, unstable emotions, and spiritual alienation are some of the ways that these imbalances might show up.

Indices of an Unbalanced Chakra:

It is essential to recognize the symptoms of chakra imbalances to determine which energy centers need to be repaired and balanced. Among the typical indications of chakra imbalances are:

Physical symptoms include immune system diseases, fatigue, gastrointestinal problems, and persistent pain.

Emotional difficulties such as worry, depression, mood changes, or trouble expressing feelings.

Addictions, poor communication, a lack of drive, or an unwillingness to set limits are examples of behavioral patterns.

Spiritual disconnection can be defined as a sense of being cut off from higher planes, lost, or disconnected from your purpose.

Chakra Healing and Balancing: Chakra healing aims to bring the chakras back into harmony and balance, allowing energy to flow freely and enhancing general wellbeing. The chakras can be balanced and healed using a variety of methods and exercises, such as:

Meditation: To purify, awaken, and harmonize the energy centers of each chakra, apply particular meditation practices.

Energy healing: Using techniques like sound healing, acupuncture, or Reiki removes blockages and brings the body's energy back into balance.

Yoga and Movement: Using poses and techniques that focus on particular chakras can assist in relieving blockages in energy and encourage flow.

Mantras and Affirmations: To rewire unfavorable mind patterns and align the chakras, recite particular mantras and use affirmations.

Crystal and Gemstone Therapy: Chakra healing and balance can be supported by harnessing the energy qualities of crystals and gemstones.

Aromatherapy: Add essential oils corresponding to each chakra to further facilitate healing.

This chapter has given you a thorough grasp of chakras, their significance, and their effects on our wellbeing, laying the foundation for your journey into chakra healing. Now that you are aware of the symptoms of chakra imbalances and have a basic understanding of healing methods, you are ready to go on to the next chapters, where we will go into greater detail about each chakra and provide you with useful exercises and meditations to help you on your healing path. Recall that chakra healing is a life-changing procedure that returns your equilibrium, harmony, and vigor and opens the door to a more contented and powerful existence.

Committing To The Heart Chakra

Our openness and capacity to experience and communicate love and compassion are attributed to the heart chakra. It all comes down to the freedom to love and be loved. We can give and accept love more easily the more open our Heart Center is. This energy center governs our relationships with others and with ourselves.

An open Heart chakra enables us to truly love ourselves and others by focusing on compassion and letting go of judgment and fear. The Root and Heart chakras are also implicated in this; what anxieties are causing you to judge other people—and maybe even yourself—in this way? These anxieties obstruct the Root chakra, and the judgmental thoughts prevent the Heart chakra from offering you the forgiveness and compassion your mind and spirit require to heal.

"This moment without judgment is inner peace. And that's it. In the Heart Center right now, anything is welcome.

— DOROTHY HUNT

The "balance point" of the seven chakras is the Heart chakra, the fourth chakra in the energy system. The Heart Chakra serves as a vital link and connection between the lower, physical/instinctual chakras (Root, Sacral, and Solar Plexus) and the higher, mental/spiritual chakras (Throat et al.), as we have discussed in earlier volumes.

The center of the chest is where the Heart chakra is situated. It is physically connected to the thymus gland, arms, lungs, heart, and chest.

There are two colors linked to the heart chakra: pink and green. Green is the primary color. Recall that the hues associated with each chakra correspond to their respective color frequencies and vibrations. The relationship between sadness, the lungs, and chest heaviness/breathing issues can be explained by the fact that the element linked with the Heart chakra is Air.

Love that is balanced is what the heart chakra is primarily there to give you.

In a spiritual sense, the heart chakra is the Source of love for oneself and others. It governs our capacity for empathy, forgiveness, and compassion.

"Empathy is the highest type of knowledge since it necessitates putting aside our egos and entering the shoes of others."

— PLATO

A light heart full of love and compassion is the gift of an open and balanced Heart chakra. Air, like love, is within and all around us. We can work to embody this element by opening our hearts and allowing love to fill and flow through us with ease. Of course, it can be unrealistic to expect to always be "full of love and compassion" because we all have our problems to work through and wounds to heal. However, this does not mean we should lack forgiveness, compassion, or love. As you work on yourself and handle your challenges at the "ego" or individual level, remember to have compassion for those around you who are healing—at their own pace.

Remember that cultivating compassion benefits you just as much as those around you. Your inner exploration and understanding of the chakras should be a source of compassion as you learn to better understand others going through the same process. Use this knowledge to nurture your feelings of compassion and assist you in letting go of any judgmental thoughts.

First Chapter

1.0 Overview of Mantra Yoga

Mantra yoga is an ancient spiritual discipline that traditional teachings of Buddhism, Hinduism, and other Eastern philosophies. It uses the power of sound vibrations to facilitate inner change and help practitioners connect with higher awareness.

Philosophy and Purpose: The fundamental idea behind Mantra Yoga is that distinct sounds, syllables, or phrases carry specific vibrational energies that have the potential to profoundly transform the mind, body, and soul of the practitioner. The ancient sages and seers discovered that by repeating these sacred sounds, people could achieve higher states of consciousness, develop mental clarity, and forge a closer bond with the divine.

Sanskrit and Sacred Languages: Mantras are typically recited in Sanskrit, an ancient language valued for strength and clarity. Nevertheless, mantras may be recited in Tibetan or Pali, depending on the spiritual tradition. Using holy languages enhances the mantras' potency because they are infused with the accumulated spiritual force from centuries of recitation by countless practitioners.

Mystical Power of Sound: In Mantra Yoga, sound affects the human mind and the external environment. The internal vibrations generated by chanting mantras resonate throughout the body, impacting multiple chakras and subtle pathways (Nadis). This resonance is believed to remove blockages to energy, purify the mind, and create a harmonic balance between the individual and the universe.

Advantages of Mantra Yoga: Regular practitioners of Mantra Yoga enjoy several noteworthy advantages, some of which are as follows:

Mental Focus and Clarity: Mantra repetition promotes mental relaxation, attentiveness, and reduced mental chatter, all contributing to improved mental focus and clarity.

Emotional Stability: Specific mantras are designed to support emotional equilibrium and well-being, assisting practitioners in managing stress, anxiety, and unpleasant feelings.

Spiritual Connection: By acting as a conduit between the individual and the divine, mantras help people feel more spiritually connected and become aware of how all life is interconnected.

Purification and Healing: Mantras' vibrational energy has the potential to clear the body's energy channels, resulting in both mental and physical healing as well as overall well-being.

Transcendence of Ego: Mantra yoga helps practitioners go beyond their limiting sense of self and experience a sense of oneness with the universe by fostering humility and transcending the ego.

Mantra Yoga in the Modern Era:

Mantra Yoga has been practiced historically in monasteries and ashrams but has also found application in modern times. People of diverse cultural backgrounds, religious perspectives, and spiritual orientations embrace Mantra Yoga as a technique for meditation and self-improvement. It has gained popularity as an adjunctive approach to stress reduction, mental health care, and overall holistic health.

To sum up, the Introduction to Mantra Yoga introduces readers to this age-old spiritual practice's essence, philosophy, and intent. It lays the foundation for the rest of the book, which explores the useful aspects, science, and applications of mantras in various areas of life.

The Role of the Seven Major Chakras

,

The Root Chakra, also called Muladhara, is the base of all seven chakras in the human body. It is symbolized by a red lotus flower with four petals, each representing a different aspect of consciousness. The Root Chakra is the starting point for growth, purity, and enlightenment. We feel grounded and secure when balanced because of its connection to the parasympathetic nervous system and adrenal glands. Imbalances can lead to anxiety, fear, and physical symptoms like lower back pain. Try yoga poses like tree pose and aromatherapy with scents like patchouli and sandalwood to find balance.

Vajra (sacramental) chakra

The second chakra in the lower abdomen is called the Sacral Chakra, or Svadhisthana. It is linked to the element of water and the color orange. It regulates reproductive health and sexual development as well as bodily functions controlled by the autonomic nervous system. Imbalances in this chakra can lead to emotional instability and physical symptoms like urinary tract infections and lower back pain. One can heal this chakra with crystals like carnelian and orange calcite, practice yoga, and meditate. The Sacral Chakra is frequently represented by a six-petaled orange lotus flower, symbolizing the six modes of consciousness: thinking, feeling, sensation, intuition, desire, and aversion.

Manipura's solar plexus chakra

is situated above the navel in the upper abdomen and is the third of the seven primary chakras in the body. An upward-pointing yellow triangle symbolizes the element fire. From a scientific standpoint, the Solar Plexus Chakra body's fight-or-flight response. It is also related to the digestive system, which includes the liver, stomach, and pancreas, as these organs break down food and generate energy for the body. Various issues, including low self-esteem, a lack of motivation, and digestive problems like indigestion and acid reflux. Meditation, yoga, and essential oils like ginger and lemon can be beneficial to restore balance to this chakra. Certain yoga poses, like plank pose and boat pose, can stimulate the Solar Plexus Chakra, promoting a healthy flow of energy, confidence, motivation, and digestive health.

Anahata, the Heart Chakra.

The Heart Chakra (also called Anahata in Sanskrit) is situated in the middle of the chest and is connected to the elements of Air and green.

Scientifically speaking, the Heart Chakra is connected to the respiratory and cardiovascular systems, which breathe in Air and distribute oxygen and other nutrients throughout the body. It is also connected to emotional qualities like love, forgiveness, and compassion, which are the core of our emotional selves and social interaction abilities.

Physical manifestations of Heart Chakra imbalances include hypertension, palpitations, and breathing problems. Emotional manifestations include trouble establishing emotional bonds, loneliness, and a lack of empathy.

The Heart Chakra can be balanced through various methods, including meditation, yoga, and aromatherapy. Specific yoga poses, such as camel and cobra, can stimulate the Heart Chakra and encourage energy flow. Essential oil-based aromatherapy, such as rose and lavender, can support emotional balance, love, and compassion.

A green lotus flower with twelve petals signifies the Heart Chakra. Different qualities of the heart are represented by each petal, which includes bliss, serenity, harmony, love, understanding, clarity, purity, compassion, forgiveness, kindness, patience, and sincerity.

the Visishuddha Chakra (throat)

It is situated at the base of the throat and is connected to the elements of ether and the color blue.

From a scientific standpoint, the respiratory and digestive systems are associated with the throat chakra because speech and communication depend heavily on the throat and vocal cords. In contrast, the digestive system breaks down food and absorbs nutrients.

The Throat Chakra is linked to honesty, integrity, and authenticity. It is in charge of efficient communication and expression through voice, writing, or other creative forms, active listening and taking in information from others.

Physical symptoms may include sore throat, thyroid difficulties, and dental concerns. Imbalances in the Throat Chakra can show up as trouble expressing oneself, speaking without regard for others, and lacking clarity or purpose in communication.

Chanting mantras like "OM" or "HAM" can stimulate and balance the energy of this chakra; singing or vocal exercises can help strengthen the throat muscles and improve communication skills; and creative expression through writing, art, or other forms of authentic self-expression. The Throat Chakra is often represented by a blue circle with 16 petals, symbolizing the 16 Sanskrit vowels associated with the chakra.

[Source]

India, Sri Lanka, and Australia.

It brings messages from the subconscious to the surface, calms an overactive mind, strengthens the imagination, enhances introspection, raises consciousness, and is a stone of transformation that is helpful during times of change. Labradorite also hinders negative energy during energy therapy and redirects unwanted energies from the aura.

Advantages

It can treat brain and eye illnesses, colds and flu, rheumatism and gout, metabolic disorders, stress reduction, blood pressure lowering, hormone balance, and PMS relief.

Positioning

You can hold it, lay it on the body as needed, or wear it as a necklace above the heart chakra.

Defense

This stone has magical and protective properties. It stops energy from leaking out of the aura, eliminates anxieties and insecurities, and removes other people's projections and thinking patterns that have slipped into the aura.

[Source]

Finland, Greenland, Italy, Scandinavia, Russia.

One of the main "love stones," sugilite opens all the chakras, grounds the soul, encourages forgiveness, especially self-forgiveness, eases grief and sorrow, and improves spiritual awareness and channeling. It is helpful when used on spiritual quests and helps to obtain answers to all the major life questions, like "Who am I?" and "Why am I here?"

Advantages

Headaches and pains can be eased; motor disturbances and epilepsy can be treated; the brain and nervous system can be aligned; the blood and lymphatic system can be purified; cancer patients' emotional turmoil can be eased; individuals with schizophrenia and paranoia can benefit; learning disabled people can benefit from it as well.

Positioning

It can be placed on the forehead to relieve headaches, on or over the heart chakra and lymph glands, or on the brow (third eye) to relieve depressive symptoms.

Defense

It absorbs bad energy, protects the soul from trauma, shock, and disappointment, eases spiritual tension, brings light into the darkest circumstances, and can help light workers and sensitive individuals adjust to the earth's vibrations.

[Source]

Japan and South Africa.

Poses of Meditation

Pose of the corpse, Savasana

Lie down in a comfortable position. Before you lie down, adjust the room's temperature. Take whatever measures you need to make yourself place a pillow under your head or over your eyes. You can place a folded towel under your knees if you have back pain.

Verify that your legs are at least hip-width apart.

- Place your arms by your sides and ensure your palms are pointing up.
- Take a deep breath, then raise your head and upper and lower extremities off the ground by tensing your entire body.
- Hold this posture briefly before releasing and exhaling through your mouth.
- Do this drill multiple times.
- Chant "Om" and see a violet light shining in your crown chakra as you do this.
- Imagine a lotus flower perched atop your head. As you breathe in, visualize heavenly white light filling the flower; as you exhale, visualize all negativity leaving your body.

After at least five minutes of stillness, resume your visualization.

Then, slowly return your attention to your breathing and move your fingers and toes to reestablish a connection with your body.

You influence the aspect of your life that controls your communication with the spiritual world every time you strike the corpse position.

www.ingramcontent.com/pod-product-compliance
Lightning Source LLC
Chambersburg PA
CBHW052134110526
44591CB00012B/1720